What is a Christian?

CAROLYN NYSTROM

Illustrated by
Wayne A. Hanna

781

MOODY PRESS
CHICAGO

MOODY PRESS
CHICAGO

© 1981 by
THE MOODY BIBLE INSTITUTE
OF CHICAGO

ISBN: 0-8024-5997-8

Printed in the United States of America

Moody Press, a ministry of the Moody Bible Institute,
is designed for education, evangelization, and
edification. If we may assist you in knowing more about
Christ and the Christian life, please write us without
obligation: Moody Press, c/o MLM, Chicago, Illinois 60610.

Jesus is my friend.
But He is more than my friend.
I belong to Jesus.

I live with my mom and dad and my
big sister, Suzy, and my baby brother, Seth.
They are my family. We take care of each
other and love each other.

I hold tools for my dad while he fixes the car,
but Dad sits behind me and pulls on my
tight boots.

I give Seth a ride on my sled, but Suzy
makes me a peanut butter sandwich for
lunch.

Once Suzy and I surprised Mom by
setting the table for supper. We picked wild
flowers for the center. But Mom cooked
the supper for us.

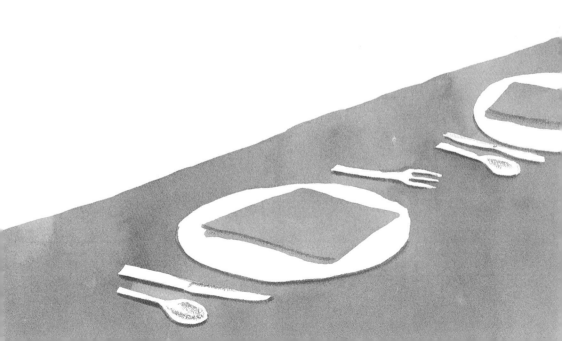

People in our family belong to each other.
I belong to Dad and Mom and Suzy and
Seth, and they belong to me.

Romans 8:14-17

But I also belong to Jesus. I am in His family, too. God is my Father. Jesus is my Brother. The Holy Spirit lives inside me.

God listens to me when I pray. I listen to God when I hear Bible stories. I obey God when I do what the Bible says.

I love Jesus and Jesus loves me. We belong together.

1 John 4:7, 19—5:2

And other people also belong in God's family. The people in God's family are special to each other.

When Mrs. Blake was sick, Mom took supper to her.

When Mr. Trooper lost his job, my dad felt sad. He helped Mr. Trooper find a new job.

When my friend Bobby won a spelling contest, I was almost as happy as he was. People in God's family care about each other because Jesus loves us all.

People in God's family are called Christians. I am a Christian. So are Mom and Dad and Mrs. Blake and Mr. Trooper and Bobby. It's great to have such a big family.

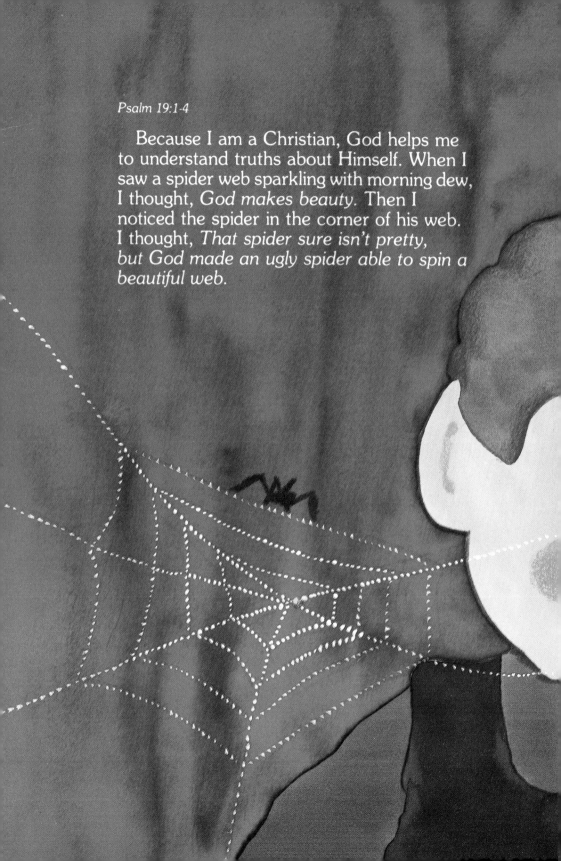

Psalm 19:1-4

Because I am a Christian, God helps me to understand truths about Himself. When I saw a spider web sparkling with morning dew, I thought, *God makes beauty.* Then I noticed the spider in the corner of his web. I thought, *That spider sure isn't pretty, but God made an ugly spider able to spin a beautiful web.*

God helps me to understand the Bible too. The Bible is like a letter from God to me, so I listen carefully to stories from the Bible.

When Mom read the story of Jesus' feeding five thousand people with five loaves and two fish, I wondered, *How did Jesus do that?* Then I thought, *If God made the whole world in the beginning, then Jesus could make bread and fish to feed only five thousand people. It shows that Jesus is God.*

God helped me understand that.

God knows everything, so He knows all about me already: what I think, what I did yesterday, what I will do tomorrow, and even when I will die. But God wants me to talk to Him anyway. People in the same family talk to each other all the time, so I pray to God every day.

I told God how sad I felt when my yellow bird died.

I told Him how much fun I had on a bike hike with Dad, and I thanked God for a sunny Saturday.

I asked God to help me fix my broken wagon, and soon I got the wagon back together.

God cares about what I do and how I feel. He wants me to ask Him for help.

When I say that I am a *Christ*ian, people know that I belong to *Christ*. The word *Christ*, another name for Jesus, is part of that name. I don't want to do anything that would cause people to think bad thoughts about Jesus. Jesus doesn't want me to do those kinds of things either. So He helps keep me from sin.

When Jesus was on earth, He never did anything wrong in His whole life. He helped people who needed help. He loved everyone, even those who were unkind to Him. He always obeyed God, His Father.

I'm not perfect, but every day Jesus is helping me live more like He did.

Philippians 2:3-11

One day, I saw a little boy roller skating. He tripped and skinned his knees. Then he sat on the sidewalk and cried. I didn't know who he was, but I asked where he lived and helped him home. Jesus would have done that, too.

Romans 12:17-21

Another time, Butch, a tough guy at school, snatched my baseball cap and threw it in a mud puddle. I felt awful. I wanted to hit him and kick him, do anything to make him feel as bad as I did. Later, I saw Butch's new baseball glove with his books. I wanted to stuff it in the garbage can just to get even. But I didn't. Jesus helped me walk away.

Colossians 3:20

The hardest part of my day is a summer
evening when it is only beginning to get dark.
Just when I am having the most fun playing,
Mom calls me home to get ready for bed.
I don't want to come at all. I want to keep
playing forever. But when I come on Mom's
first call, it is Jesus who helps me obey.

If I come fast, we have time for a story—
and I'm glad I came.

But I do not always do what Jesus wants.
Sometimes I yank toys from Seth.
I stomp on Bobby's new truck.
I yell, "No!" at my mom.
I feel sad after I do those things; I know that Jesus feels sad too. I say, "Jesus, I'm sorry. I'll try not to do it again."
And Jesus forgives me. He always will.

John 3:16; Romans 5:8

Jesus knows that I am not perfect.
That's why He came to earth. He was perfect
—even if I cannot be. So He died on a cross
to take the punishment for all the things
I do wrong. He invites me into His family. It's
hard to understand how Jesus loves me
that much. But He does.

John 10:27-30; 14:1-3

And Jesus will never, never leave me alone.
I am in His family forever.

Even now Jesus is making heaven ready
for me and for all the others in His family.
After we die, we will all live in heaven
with Jesus. And heaven is forever.

Would you like to be a Christian? If so, you can belong to Jesus, too. There are three things you need to do.

Isaiah 59:1-2; 1 John 1:9

1. *Think.* Remember the things you have done wrong. Have you ever told a lie? Taken something that was not yours? Disobeyed your mom or dad? The things that we do wrong are called sins. Any sin separates us from God.

Say, "Jesus, I'm sorry for all the things I've done wrong."

2. *Believe.* Believe that Jesus died and came back to life to forgive those sins and take them away forever.

Say, "Thank you, Jesus. I believe You took the punishment for all the things I do wrong."

3. *Decide.* Do you really want to belong to Jesus? If you do, that means that you will let Jesus be in charge of all that you do.
(You will pray often. You will learn from the Bible and try as hard as you can to obey it. Whenever you do something wrong, you will tell Jesus you are sorry. And you will try to make it up to anyone that you hurt.)

Romans 12:1

If you decide that you want to belong to Jesus, say, "Jesus, I give You myself. I want to belong to You forever."

John 6:35-37; Revelation 3:20

If you take those three steps, then you are a Christian. You may not feel different, but that doesn't matter. Jesus loves you and forgives you. The Bible says that Jesus accepts anyone who comes to Him.

In God's family, there is always room.
Welcome to the family.